Korean Alphabet

with

Writing Workbook

Introductory Guide To Hangeul Series
Vol. 1: Vowel and Consonant
자음과 모음

NABI PUBLISHING

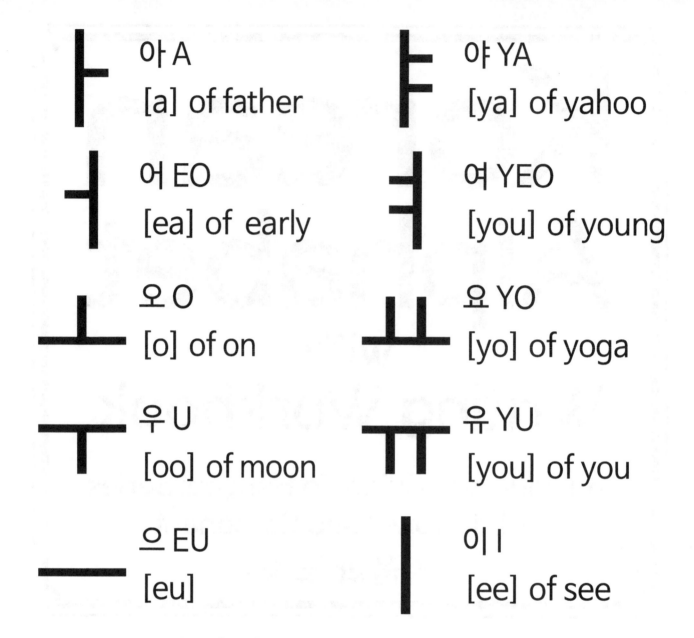

ㅏ 아 A
[a] of father

ㅑ 야 YA
[ya] of yahoo

ㅓ 어 EO
[ea] of early

ㅕ 여 YEO
[you] of young

ㅗ 오 O
[o] of on

ㅛ 요 YO
[yo] of yoga

ㅜ 우 U
[oo] of moon

ㅠ 유 YU
[you] of you

ㅡ 으 EU
[eu]

ㅣ 이 I
[ee] of see

Korean vowel —[eu] sound is not used in English as a distinct sound but is close to a passing sound. Here are a few examples where you can find a hint of the 으 [eu] sound with English words in Korean writing.

Slide → [슬라이드 seul-la-i-deu]
Space → [스페이스 seu-pe-i-seu]
Sandwich → [샌드위치 saen-deu-wi-chi]

ㄱ 기역 [gi-yeok]
[g] of gate

ㄴ 니은 [ni-eun]
[n] of nail

ㄷ 디귿 [di-geut]
[d] of dog

ㄹ 리을 [ri-eul]
[l] of lemon

ㅁ 미음 [mi-eum]
[m] of mom

ㅂ 비읍 [bi-eup]
[b] of bear

ㅅ 시옷 [si-ot]
[s] of snail

ㅇ 이응 [i-eung]
-/[ng] of king

ㅈ 지읒 [ji-eut]
[j] of jelly

ㅊ 치읓 [chi-eut]
[ch] of child

ㅋ 키읔 [ki-euk]
[k] of kiwi

ㅌ 티읕 [ti-eut]
[t] of table

ㅍ 피읖 [pi-eup]
[p] of penguin

ㅎ 히읗 [hi-eut]
[h] of house

ㅐ 애 AE
[a] of bad

ㅒ 얘 YAE
[ya] of yam

ㅔ 에 E
[e] of bed

ㅖ 예 YE
[ye] of yes

ㅘ 와 WA
[wha] of what

ㅙ 왜 WAE
[wa] of wagon

ㅚ 외 OE
[we] of wedding

ㅝ 워 WO
[wa] of want

ㅞ 웨 WE
[we] of wedding

ㅟ 위 WI
[wi] of kiwi

ㅢ 의 UI
ㅡ + ㅣ [eui]

Vowel ㅢ does not have a similar sound in English

In modern Korean, ㅚ is pronounced the same as ㅞ.

ㄲ 쌍기역 [ssang-gi-yeok]
[kk]

ㄸ 쌍디귿 [ssang-di-geut]
[tt]

ㅃ 쌍비읍 [ssang-bi-eup]
[pp]

ㅆ 쌍시옷 [ssang-si-ot]
[ss] s of sun

ㅉ 쌍지읒 [ssang-ji-eut]
[jj]

Practice pages and detailed information on complex vowels and double consonants are in the next book 'Korean Alphabet with Writing Workbook: Introductory Guide To Hangeul Series Vol. 2'

모음 Vowel

ㅏ	ㅓ	ㅗ	ㅜ	ㅡ
ㅑ	ㅕ	ㅛ	ㅠ	ㅣ

자음 Consonant

ㄱ	ㄴ	ㄷ	ㄹ	ㅁ	ㅂ	ㅅ
ㅇ	ㅈ	ㅊ	ㅋ	ㅌ	ㅍ	ㅎ

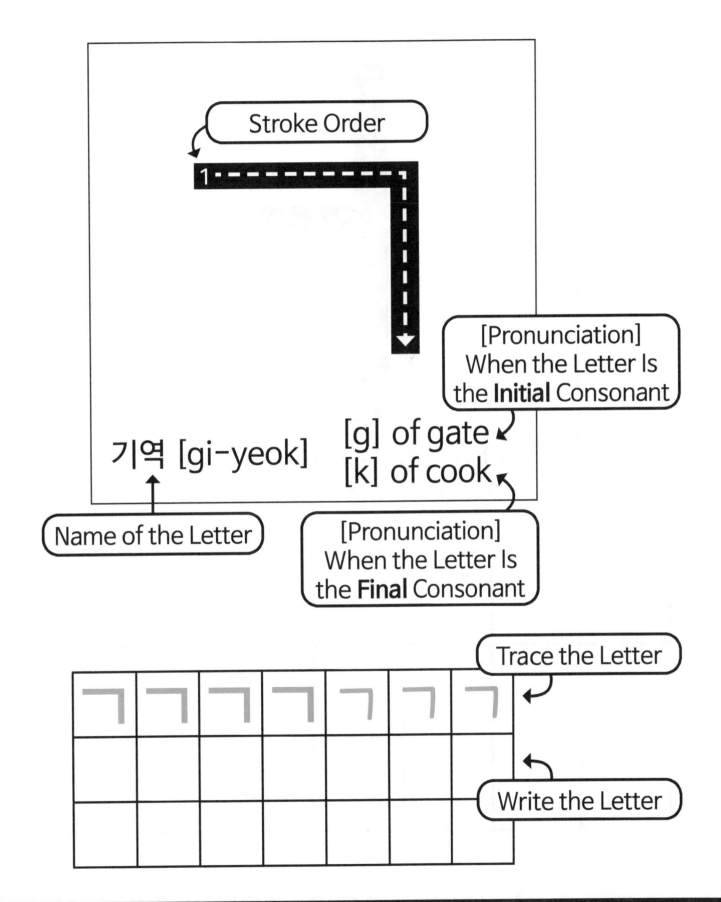

Stroke Order

1

[Pronunciation]
When the Letter Is
the **Initial** Consonant

[g] of gate
[k] of cook

기역 [gi-yeok]

Name of the Letter

[Pronunciation]
When the Letter Is
the **Final** Consonant

Trace the Letter

Write the Letter

아 A   [a] of Avocado

ㅏ	ㅏ	ㅏ	ㅏ	아	아	아

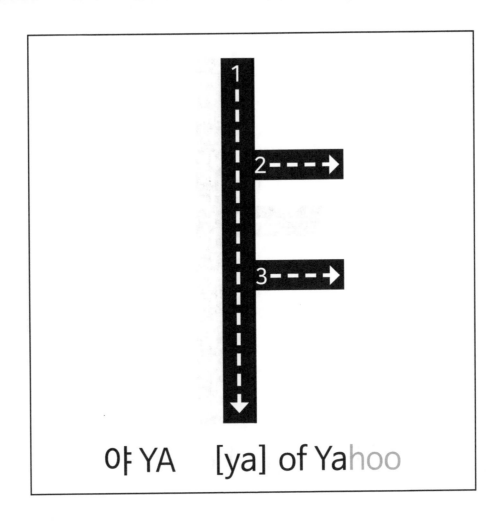

야 YA   [ya] of Yahoo

ㅑ	ㅑ	ㅑ	ㅑ	야	야	야

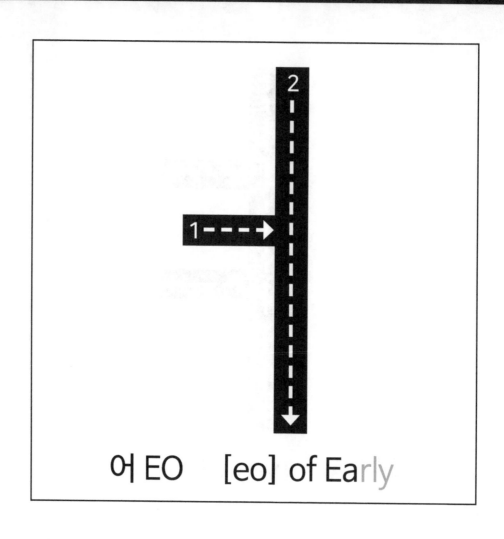

어 EO   [eo] of Early

ㅓ	ㅓ	ㅓ	ㅓ	어	어	어

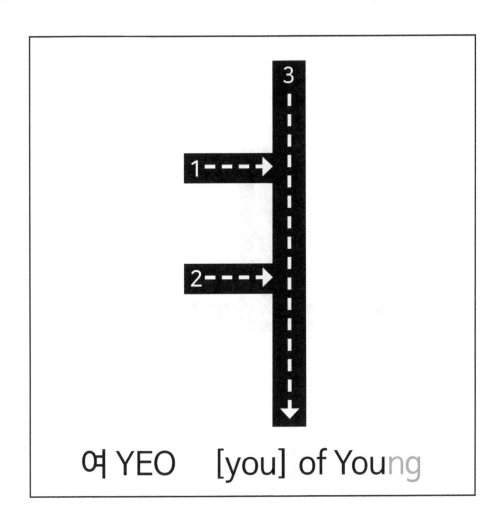

여 YEO   [you] of Young

ㅕ	ㅕ	ㅕ	ㅕ	여	여	여

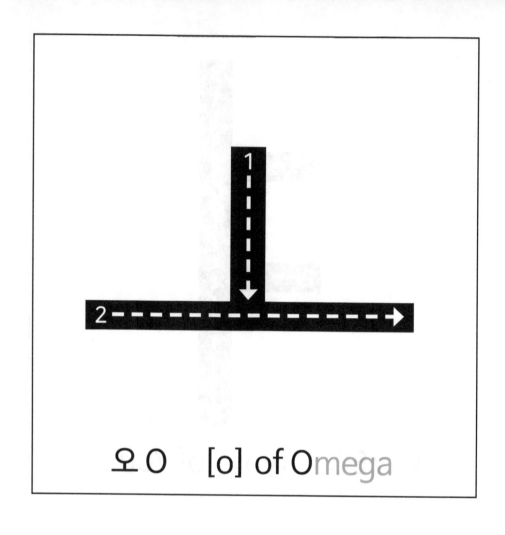

오 O   [o] of Omega

⊥	⊥	⊥	⊥	오	오	오

요 YO   [yo] of Yoga

ㅛ	ㅛ	ㅛ	ㅛ	요	요	요

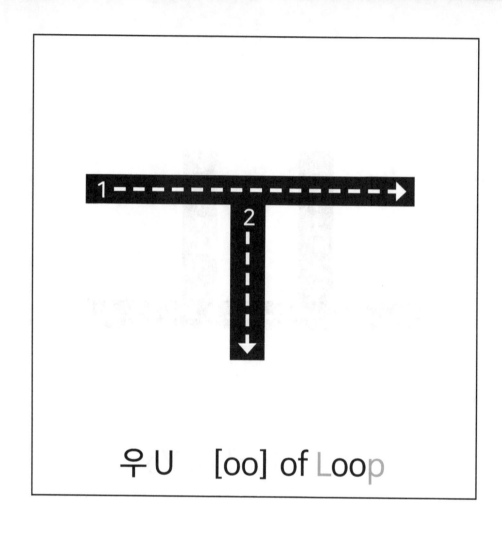

우 U   [oo] of Loop

ㅜ	ㅜ	ㅜ	ㅜ	우	우	우

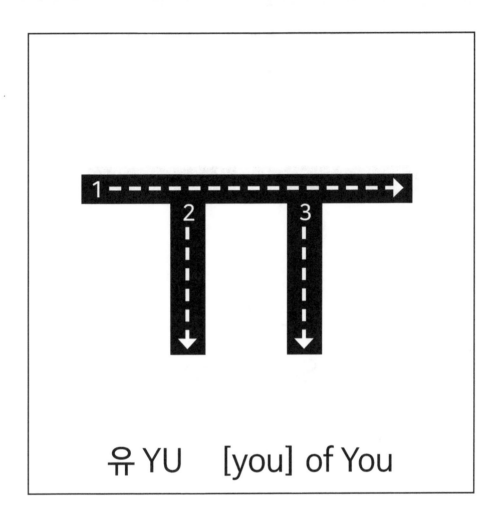

유 YU   [you] of You

ㅠ	ㅠ	ㅠ	ㅠ	유	유	유

1 - - - - - - - - - - - - →

으 EU

Sandwich
샌드위치
[saen-deu-wi-chi]

ㅡ	ㅡ	ㅡ	ㅡ	으	으	으

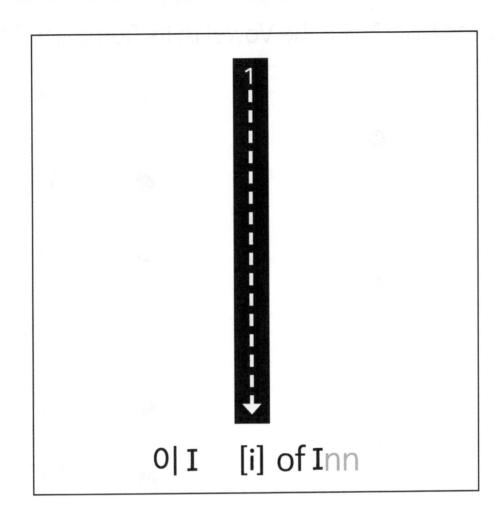

0| I   [i] of Inn

						O	O	O

Connect the Dots From the Vowel to Its Romanized Name.

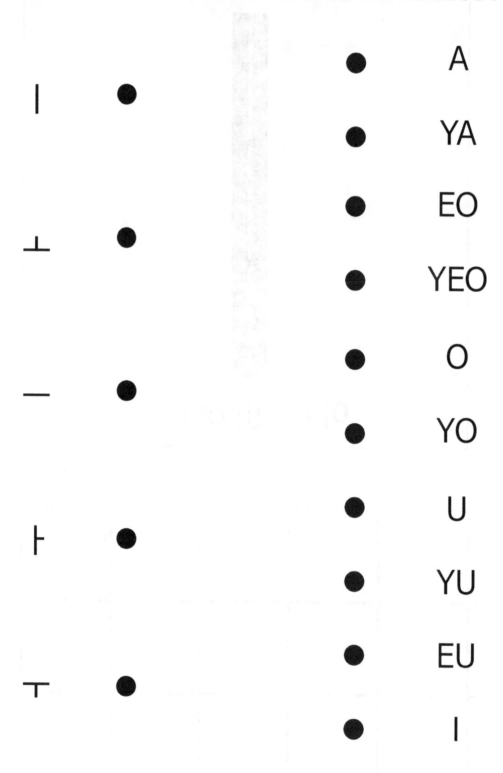

ㅑ ●

ㅓ ●

ㅕ ●

ㅛ ●

ㅠ ●

● A

● EO

● O

● U

● YA

● YO

● YU

● YEO

● EU

● I

ㅏ	ㅑ	ㅓ	ㅕ	ㅗ	ㅛ	ㅜ	ㅠ	ㅡ	ㅣ
ㅏ	ㅑ	ㅓ	ㅕ	ㅗ	ㅛ	ㅜ	ㅠ	ㅡ	ㅣ
ㅏ	ㅑ	ㅓ	ㅕ	ㅗ	ㅛ	ㅜ	ㅠ	ㅡ	ㅣ

ㅏ	ㅑ	ㅓ	ㅕ	ㅗ	ㅛ	ㅜ	ㅠ	ㅡ	ㅣ

아	야	어	여	오	요	우	유	으	이
아	야	어	여	오	요	우	유	으	이
아	야	어	여	오	요	우	유	으	이
아	야	어	여	오	요	우	유	으	이
아	야	어	여	오	요	우	유	으	이
아	야	어	여	오	요	우	유	으	이
아	야	어	여	오	요	우	유	으	이

아	야	어	여	오	요	우	유	으	이

Syllabic Block

Korean letters are combined to form syllabic blocks. A syllabic block is composed of a consonant(s) and a vowel. There are two types of syllabic blocks, C+V and C+V+C. The first/initial consonant is the starting letter of the block. And the final consonant (받침 batchim) is the last consonant of the C+V+C block. Every syllabic block must contain the initial consonant and a vowel; some blocks contain the final consonant.

Initial Consonant

C + V = CV
Consonant   Vowel

Final Consonant
(받침 Batchim)

Initial Consonant

C + V + C = CVC
Consonant   Vowel   Consonant

Different Shapes of Syllabic Blocks

CV → 가 → 가

C V / C → 각 → 각

C / V → 고 → 고

C / V / C → 곡 → 곡

Most Korean consonants have different pronunciations depending on the position inside the syllabic block, which means whether the consonant is used as the initial or final consonant determines the sound. When you look at the romanized name of each consonant, it contains information for the initial and final consonant sounds.

For example, the name of the letter ㄱ is 기역 Giyeo**K**. As an **initial** consonant, it sounds like the **g** of gate. As a **final** consonant, it sounds like the **k** of cook.

ㄱ + ㅏ = 가
g   a   ga

ㄱ + ㅏ + ㄱ = 각
g   a   k   gak

Some consonants have the same sound in both positions. For example, the letter ㄴ 니은 **NieuN** sounds like the **n** of noon as the initial and final consonant.

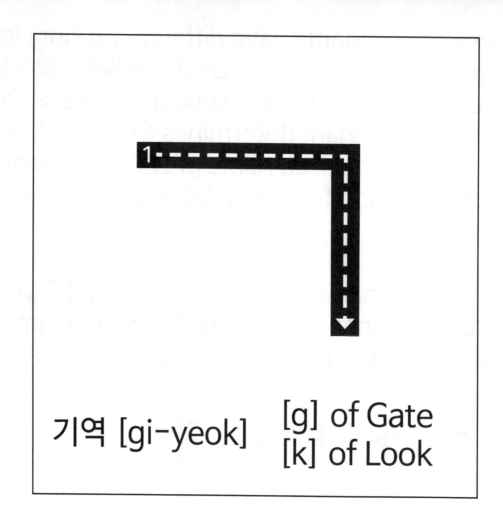

기역 [gi-yeok] [g] of Gate
[k] of Look

고양이
[go-yang-i]
Cat

곰
[gom]
Bear

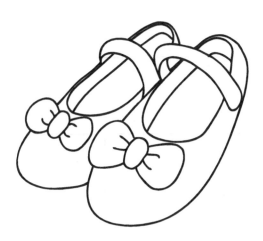

구두
[gu-du]
Shoes

구름
[gu-reum]
Cloud

ㄱ ㄱ ㄱ ㄱ ㄱ ㄱ ㄱ ㄱ

고양이

고	양	이	고	양	이

곰

곰	곰

구두

구	두	구	두

구름

구	름	구	름

니은 [ni-eun]   [n] of Noon

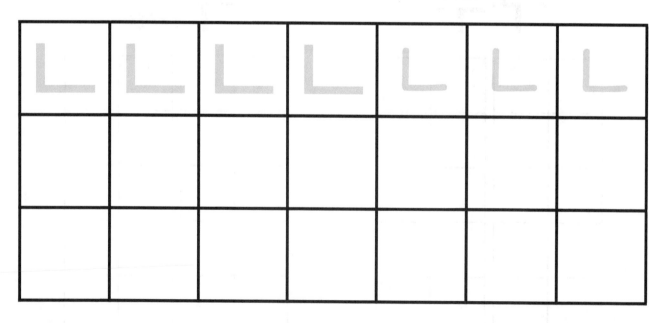

나비
[na-bi]
Butterfly

낙타
[nak-ta]
Camel

나무
[na-mu]
Tree

눈사람
[nun-sa-ram]
Snowman

L L L L L L L L L

눈사람

눈	사	람	눈	사	람

나비

나	비	나	비

낙타

낙	타	낙	타

나무

나	무	나	무

고양이 ●

●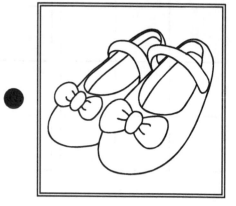

곰 ●

●

구두 ●

구름 ● ●

나비 ●

낙타 ●

나무 ●

눈사람 ●

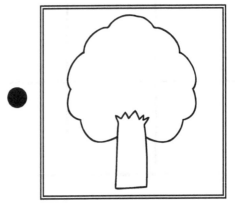

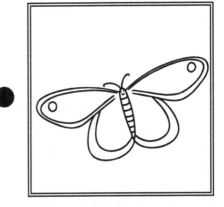

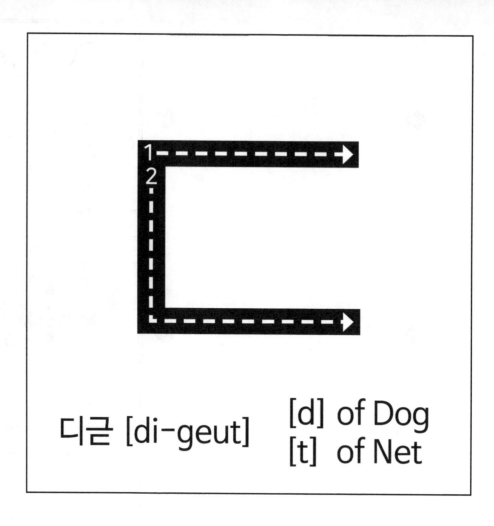

ㄷㄷㄷ [di-geut]   [d] of Dog
[t] of Net

ㄷ	ㄷ	ㄷ	ㄷ	ㄷ	ㄷ	ㄷ

다리
[da-ri]
Bridge

다리미
[da-ri-mi]
Iron

다람쥐
[da-ram-jwi]
Squirrel

당근
[dang-geun]
Carrot

ㄷ ㄷ ㄷ ㄷ ㄷ ㄷ ㄷ ㄷ

다 더 러 려 르 므 브 쓰 으 ㅈ

다리미　다리

다	리	미	다	리	미

다	리	다	리

다람쥐　당근

다	람	쥐	다	람	쥐

당	근	당	근

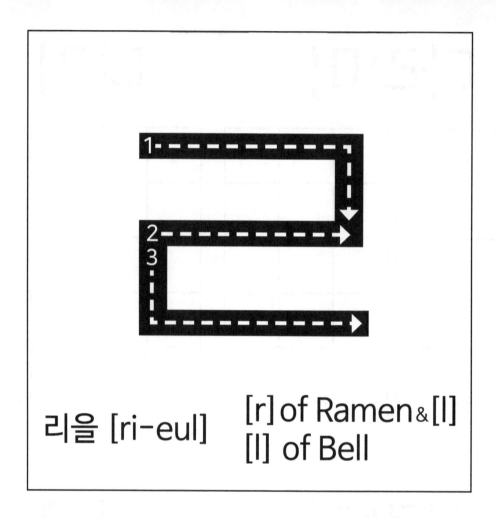

리을 [ri-eul]   [r] of Ramen & [l]
[l] of Bell

레몬
[le-mon]
Lemon

리본
[li-bon]
Ribbon

로봇
[lo-bot]
Robot

라디오
[la-di-o]
Radio

2 2 2 2 2 2 2 2

라디오

라	디	오	라	디	오

로봇

로	봇	로	봇

리본

리	본	리	본

레몬

레	몬	레	몬

다리 ● ●

당근 ● ●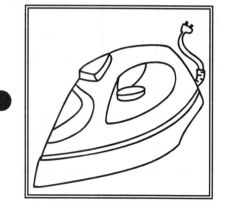

다리미 ● ●

다람쥐 ● ●

레몬 ●　　　　●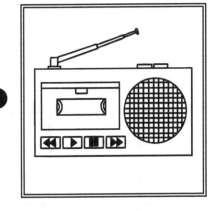

리본 ●　　　　●

로봇 ●　　　　●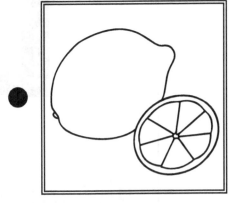

라디오 ●　　　　●

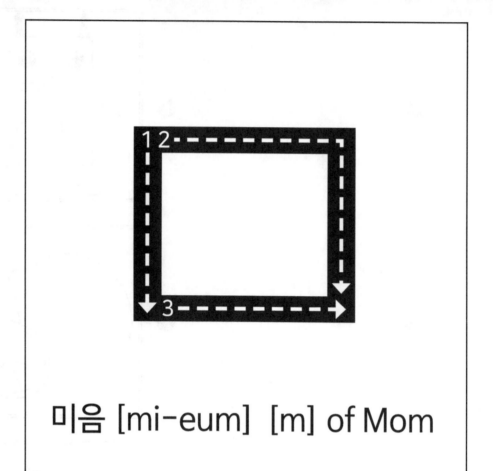

미음 [mi-eum] [m] of Mom

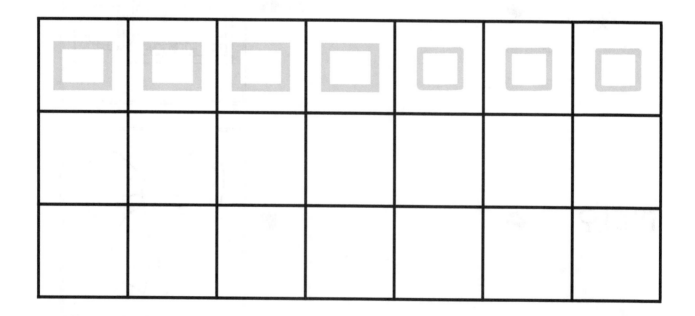

마늘
[ma-neul]
Garlic

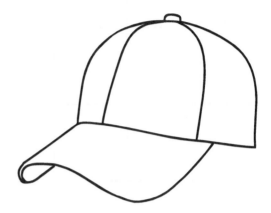

모자
[mo-ja]
Hat

마이크
[ma-i-keu]
Mike

말
[mal]
Horse

아 야 어 여 오

요 우 유 으 이

50

마이크

마	이	크	마	이	크

말

말	말

모자

모	자	모	자

마늘

마	늘	마	늘

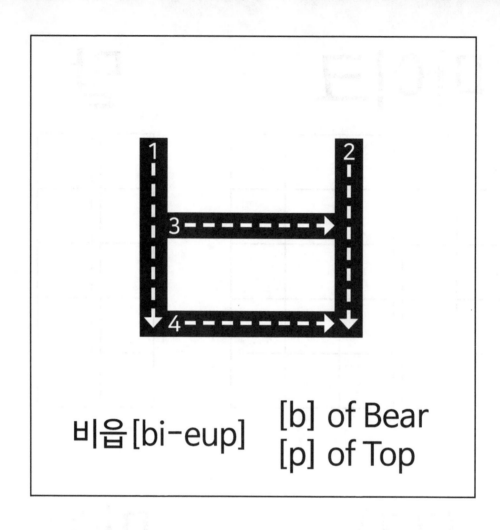

비읍[bi-eup]   [b] of Bear
                [p] of Top

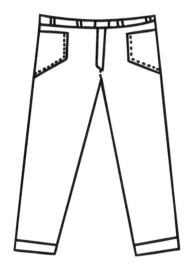

바지
[ba-ji]
Pants

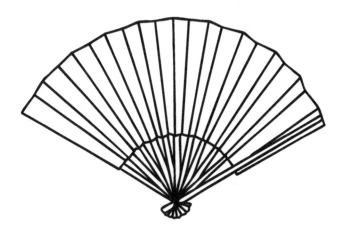

부채
[bu-chae]
Fan

바나나
[ba-na-na]
Banana

버섯
[beo-seot]
Mushroom

ㅂ ㅂ ㅂ ㅂ ㅂ ㅂ ㅂ ㅂ

바 뱌 버 벼 보

뵤 부 뷰 브 비

바나나

바	나	나	바	나	나

바지

바	지	바	지

부채

부	채	부	채

버섯

버	섯	버	섯

마늘 ●

●

모자 ●

●

마이크 ●

●

말 ●

●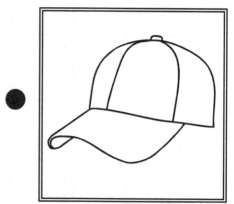

바지　●

●　

부채　●

바나나　●

●　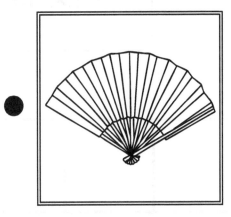

버섯　●

●　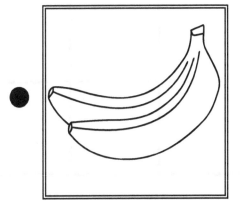

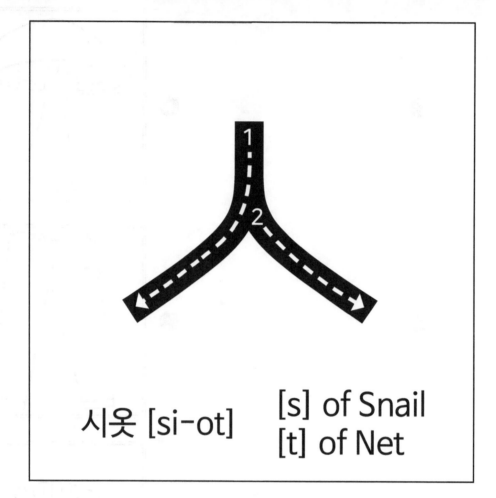

시옷 [si-ot]   [s] of Snail
[t] of Net

수박
[su-bak]
Watermelon

사자
[sa-ja]
Lion

사탕
[sa-tang]
Candy

시계
[si-gye]
Clock

人	人	人	人	人	人	人	人

사	사	서	서	소
솜	수	수	시	시

수박

수	박	수	박

사자

사	자	사	자

사탕

사	탕	사	탕

시계

시	계	시	계

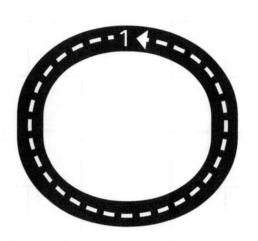

이응 [i-eung]   Silent/No Sound
[ng] of Sing

O	O	O	O	O	O	O

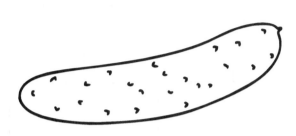

오이
[o-i]
Cucumber

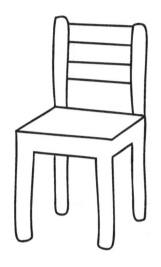

의자
[ui-ja]
Chair

우산
[u-san]
Umbrella

우표
[u-pyo]
Stamp

○	○	○	○	○	○	○	○

아	야	어	여	오
요	우	유	으	이

오이

오	이	오	이

의자

의	자	의	자

우산

우	산	우	산

우표

우	표	우	표

수박 ●

●

사자 ●

●

사탕 ●

●

시계 ●

●

오이   ●   ●

의자   ●   ●

우산   ●   ●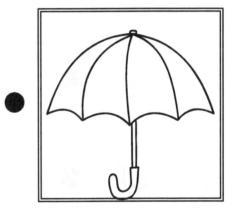

우표   ●   ●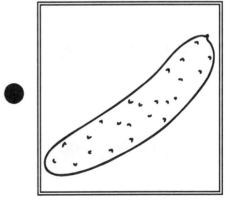

Connect the Dots

Connect the Dots From the Letter's Name to the Letter.

NI-EUN ●   ● ㄷ

                ● ㄱ

DI-GEUT ●   ● ㄹ

SI-OT ●   ● ㅁ

                ● ㅋ

MI-EUM ●   ● ㄴ

RI-EUL ●   ● ㅎ

BI-EUP ●   ● ㅅ

                ● ㅈ

I-EUNG ●   ● ㅇ

GI-YEOK ●   ● ㅂ

Beginning Sounds

Color the Circle That Contains the Beginning Sound of the Picture.

7 7 7 7 7 7 7

L L L L L L L

⊏ ⊏ ⊏ ⊏ ⊏ ⊏ ⊏

2 2 2 2 2 2 2

ㅁ	ㅁ	ㅁ	ㅁ	ㅁ	ㅁ	ㅁ

ㅂ	ㅂ	ㅂ	ㅂ	ㅂ	ㅂ	ㅂ

ㅅ	ㅅ	ㅅ	ㅅ	ㅅ	ㅅ	ㅅ

ㅇ	ㅇ	ㅇ	ㅇ	ㅇ	ㅇ	ㅇ

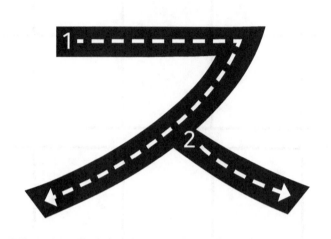

지읒 [ji-eut]　[j] of Jelly
[t] of Net

ス	ス	ス	ス	ス	ス	ス

자전거
[ja-jeon-geo]
Bicycle

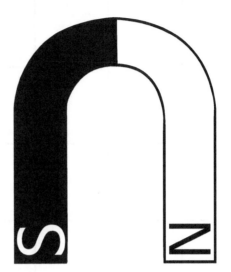

자석
[ja-seok]
Magnet

자동차
[ja-dong-cha]
Car

주전자
[ju-jeon-ja]
Kettle

ス	ス	ス	ス	ス	ス	ス	ス

사	서	저	져	조
좀	주	즈	즈	지

자전거

자	전	거	자	전	거

자석

자	석	자	석

자동차

자	동	차	자	동	차

주전자

주	전	자

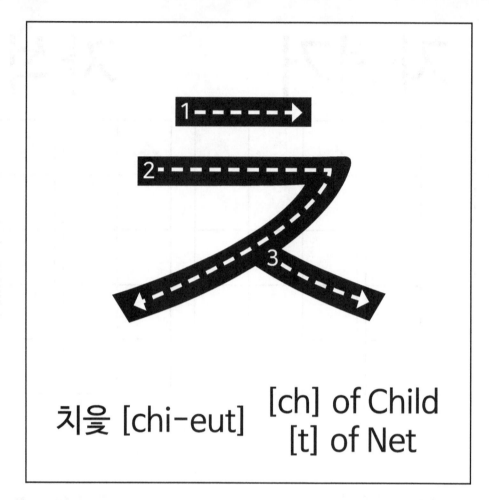

치읓 [chi-eut]   [ch] of Child
[t] of Net

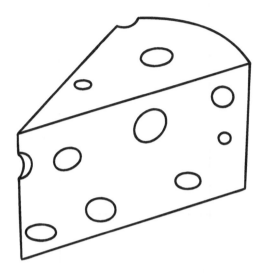

치즈
[chi-jeu]
Cheese

치마
[chi-ma]
Skirt

치약
[chi-yak]
Toothpaste

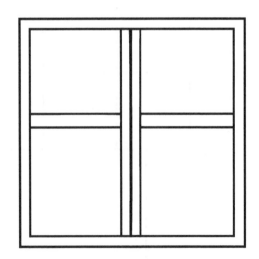

창문
[chang-mun]
Window

ス　ス　ス　ス　ス　ス　ス　ス

치즈

치	즈	치	즈

치마

치	마	치	마

치약

치	약	치	약

창문

창	문	창	문

자전거 ● ●

자석 ● ●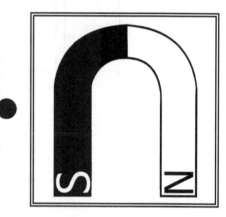

자동차 ● ●

주전자 ● ●

치즈 ●   ●

치마 ●   ●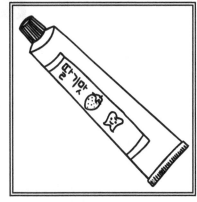

치약 ●   ●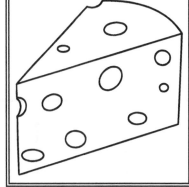

창문 ●   ●

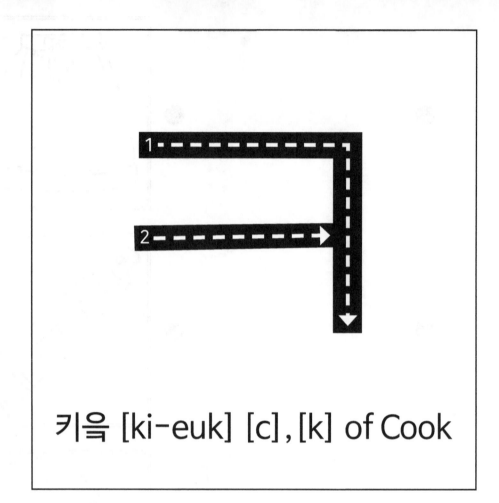

키읔 [ki-euk] [c],[k] of Cook

ㅋ ㅋ ㅋ ㅋ ㅋ ㅋ ㅋ

코끼리
[ko-kki-ri]
Elephant

카메라
[ka-me-ra]
Camera

컴퓨터
[keom-pu-teo]
Computer

키위
[ki-wi]
Kiwi

ㅋ ㅋ ㅋ ㅋ ㅋ ㅋ ㅋ ㅋ

카 캐 켜 켸 코

쿄 쿠 큐 크 키

코끼리

코	끼	리	코	끼	리

키위

키	위	키	위

카메라

카	메	라	카	메	라

컴퓨터

컴	퓨	터

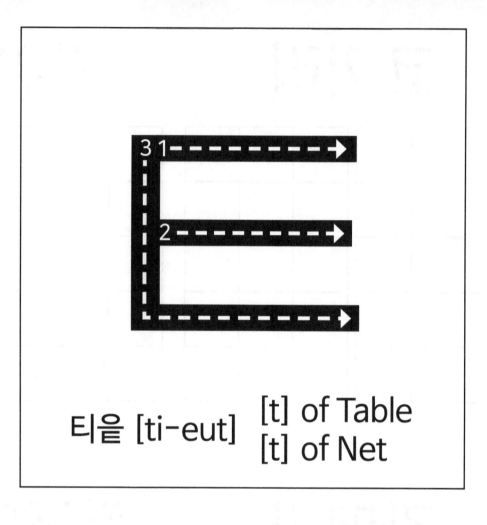

티읕 [ti-eut]   [t] of Table
[t] of Net

토끼
[to-kki]
Rabbit

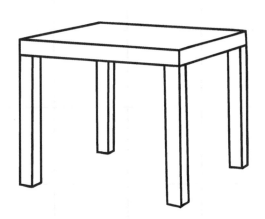

탁자
[tak-ja]
Table

토마토
[to-ma-to]
Tomato

타조
[ta-jo]
Ostrich

E	E	E	E	E	E	E	E

토마토

토	마	토	토	마	토

토끼

토	끼	토	끼

탁자

탁	자	탁	자

타조

타	조	타	조

코끼리 ●

●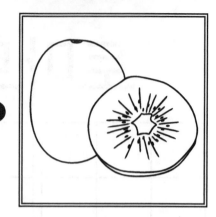

카메라 ●

●

컴퓨터 ●

●

키위 ●

●

토끼 ●

●

탁자 ●

●

토마토 ●

●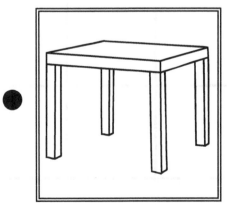

타조 ●

●

피읖 [pi-eup]   [p] of Panda
[p] of Top

포도
[po-do]
Grape

편지
[pyeon-ji]
Letter

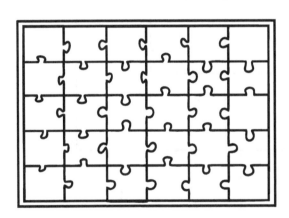

퍼즐
[peo-jeul]
Puzzle

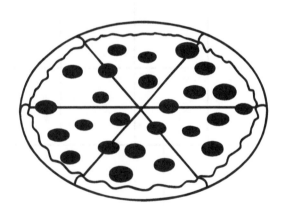

피자
[pi-ja]
Pizza

ㅍ	ㅍ	ㅍ	ㅍ	ㅍ	ㅍ	ㅍ	ㅍ

파	퍄	퍼	펴	표
푸	퓨	프	피	파

포도

포	도	포	도

편지

편	지	편	지

퍼즐

퍼	즐	퍼	즐

피자

피	자	피	자

히읗 [hi-eut]

[h] of House
[t] of Net

호박
[ho-bak]
Pumpkin

해바라기
[hae-ba-ra-gi]
Sunflower

해
[hae]
Sun

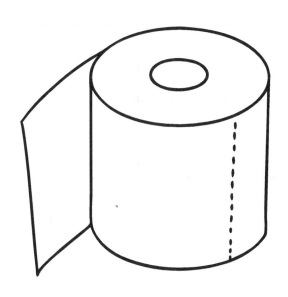

휴지
[hyu-ji]
Toilet Paper

ㅎ ㅎ ㅎ ㅎ ㅎ ㅎ ㅎ ㅎ

하 햐 허 혀 호

효 후 휴 흐 히

해바라기 　 해

해	바	라	기	해	바	라	기

해	해

휴지 　 호박

휴	지	휴	지

호	박	호	박

포도 ●  ●

편지 ●  ●

퍼즐 ● 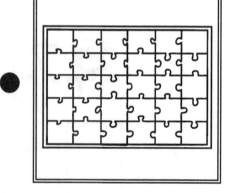 ●

피자 ● 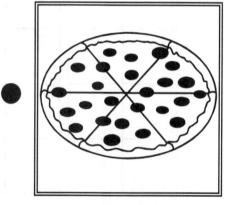 ●

호박 ●　　　　　　●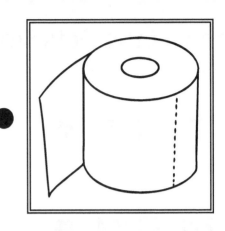

해바라기 ●　　　　　　●

해 ●　　　　　　●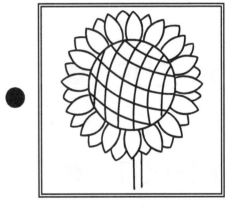

휴지 ●　　　　　　●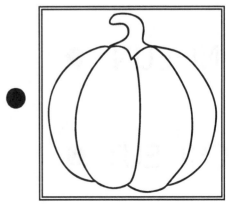

Connect the Dots

Connect the Dots From the Letter's Name to the Letter.

TI-EUT ●   ● ㄷ

                    ● ㄱ

MI-EUM ●   ● ㅊ

JI-EUT ●   ● ㅁ

KI-EUK ●   ● ㅋ

                    ● ㄴ

PI-EUP ●   ● ㅎ

HI-EUT ●   ● ㅍ

                    ● ㅈ

NI-EUN ●   ● ㅌ

CHI-EUT ●   ● ㅂ

Color the Circle That Contains the Beginning Sound of the Picture.

ス	ス	ス	ス	ス	ス	ス

ㅈ	ㅈ	ㅈ	ㅈ	ㅈ	ㅈ	ㅈ

ㅋ	ㅋ	ㅋ	ㅋ	ㅋ	ㅋ	ㅋ

ㅌ	ㅌ	ㅌ	ㅌ	ㅌ	ㅌ	ㅌ

ㅍ	ㅍ	ㅍ	ㅍ	ㅍ	ㅍ	ㅍ

ㅎ	ㅎ	ㅎ	ㅎ	ㅎ	ㅎ	ㅎ

ㄱ	ㄴ	ㄷ	ㄹ	ㅁ	ㅂ	ㅅ

ㅇ	ㅈ	ㅊ	ㅋ	ㅌ	ㅍ	ㅎ

ㄱ										
ㄴ										
ㄷ										
ㄹ										
ㅁ										
ㅂ										
ㅅ										
ㅇ										
ㅈ										
ㅊ										
ㅋ										
ㅌ										
ㅍ										
ㅎ										

ㄱ										
ㄴ										
ㄷ										
ㄹ										
ㅁ										
ㅂ										
ㅅ										
ㅇ										
ㅈ										
ㅊ										
ㅋ										
ㅌ										
ㅍ										
ㅎ										

GI-YEOK		I-EUNG	
NI-EUN		JI-EUT	
DI-GEUT		CHI-EUT	
RI-EUL		KI-EUK	
MI-EUM		TI-EUT	
BI-EUP		PI-EUP	
SI-OT		HI-EUT	

A			YO	

YA			U	

EO			YU	

YEO			EU	

O			I	

	ㅏ	ㅑ	ㅓ	ㅕ	ㅗ	ㅛ	ㅜ	ㅠ	ㅡ	ㅣ
ㄱ	가									
ㄴ			너							
ㄷ					도					
ㄹ							루			
ㅁ									므	
ㅂ		뱌								
ㅅ				셔						
ㅇ						요				
ㅈ								쥬		
ㅊ										치
ㅋ										
ㅌ										
ㅍ										
ㅎ										

	ㅏ	ㅑ	ㅓ	ㅕ	ㅗ	ㅛ	ㅜ	ㅠ	ㅡ	ㅣ
ㄱ										
ㄴ										
ㄷ										
ㄹ										
ㅁ										
ㅂ										
ㅅ										
ㅇ										
ㅈ										
ㅊ										
ㅋ										
ㅌ										
ㅍ										
ㅎ										

	ㅏ	ㅑ	ㅓ	ㅕ	ㅗ	ㅛ	ㅜ	ㅠ	ㅡ	ㅣ
ㄱ										
ㄴ										
ㄷ										
ㄹ										
ㅁ										
ㅂ										
ㅅ										
ㅇ										
ㅈ										
ㅊ										
ㅋ										
ㅌ										
ㅍ										
ㅎ										

	ㅏ	ㅑ	ㅓ	ㅕ	ㅗ	ㅛ	ㅜ	ㅠ	ㅡ	ㅣ
ㄱ										
ㄴ										
ㄷ										
ㄹ										
ㅁ										
ㅂ										
ㅅ										
ㅇ										
ㅈ										
ㅊ										
ㅋ										
ㅌ										
ㅍ										
ㅎ										

	ㅏ	ㅑ	ㅓ	ㅕ	ㅗ	ㅛ	ㅜ	ㅠ	ㅡ	ㅣ
ㄱ										
ㄴ										
ㄷ										
ㄹ										
ㅁ										
ㅂ										
ㅅ										
ㅇ										
ㅈ										
ㅊ										
ㅋ										
ㅌ										
ㅍ										
ㅎ										

	ㅏ	ㅑ	ㅓ	ㅕ	ㅗ	ㅛ	ㅜ	ㅠ	ㅡ	ㅣ
ㄱ										
ㄴ										
ㄷ										
ㄹ										
ㅁ										
ㅂ										
ㅅ										
ㅇ										
ㅈ										
ㅊ										
ㅋ										
ㅌ										
ㅍ										
ㅎ										

	ㅏ	ㅑ	ㅓ	ㅕ	ㅗ	ㅛ	ㅜ	ㅠ	ㅡ	ㅣ
ㄱ										
ㄴ										
ㄷ										
ㄹ										
ㅁ										
ㅂ										
ㅅ										
ㅇ										
ㅈ										
ㅊ										
ㅋ										
ㅌ										
ㅍ										
ㅎ										

	ㅏ	ㅑ	ㅓ	ㅕ	ㅗ	ㅛ	ㅜ	ㅠ	ㅡ	ㅣ
ㄱ										
ㄴ										
ㄷ										
ㄹ										
ㅁ										
ㅂ										
ㅅ										
ㅇ										
ㅈ										
ㅊ										
ㅋ										
ㅌ										
ㅍ										
ㅎ										

Made in United States
Troutdale, OR
05/07/2024

19690306R00066